Lead BOLDLY. Live FULLY

Lead BOLDLY. Live FULLY

A Leadership Fable

By Anisa Rashad, MBA
Founder & CEO, ARE Global Solutions

Lead BOLDLY. Live FULLY

Published by ARE Global Media Group
Tampa, FL

www.areglobalsolutions.com
www.leadboldlylivefully.net

ISBN: 979-8-9988006-0-3

Cover design and interior formatting by Little Folk Stories

First Edition, 2026
Printed in the United States of America on cream-colored paper

Contents

Acknowledgments

"When did you first fall in love with hip hop?" That's the question that opens the movie "Brown Sugar."

So let me ask it my way: When did I first fall in love with leadership?

I fell in love with leadership the first time I was trained to facilitate a Franklin Planner class in the '90s. There was something about helping people align their time with their values that lit a fire in me—and it's never gone out.

To my ARE Global Solutions team—Thank you for being the architects of our impact.

To our Clients—Thank you for trusting us with your growth, your leadership, and your legacy.

To the CHROs and talent leaders who open the door for transformation in their organizations—Your belief in people-first leadership is changing the game.

To my Parents—Your unconditional love and belief in me continue to light my path and shape my purpose. (Greatest parents EVERRRRR)

To my Heartbeats—Jahari, Zuri, and Malik—You are my joy and my reason.

To my Sister—You are a lifelong gift of love, laughter, and unwavering support.

To my Ancestors—You are my wisdom and my walk.

To God—Thank you for choosing me, equipping me, and holding me through every chapter.

This book is for the leader whose outer success hides an inner longing for something more real, more fulfilling, more whole.

It's an invitation for you to Lead BOLDLY and Live FULLY!

Introduction

Welcome, Beautiful Leader—

If you're reading this, I already know one thing about you:

You are someone who is ready to stop simply *functioning* and start *fully living*.

This book is more than a story. It is an invitation.

To pause. To reflect. To realign.

To remember that your time, energy, and attention are sacred.

To reclaim the truth that your leadership and your life don't have to compete.

They can *coexist*, beautifully.

As the Founder and CEO of ARE Global Solutions, I've had the honor of coaching powerful leaders across the globe—and I've seen one truth hold: You don't have to lose yourself to lead others.

Let this book support you in becoming a TEAM—a Time, Energy, and Attention Manager™.

Let your calendar reflect your values.

Let your joy take up space.

Let your essence lead the way.

You are worth investing in.

Your leadership matters.

And you already have everything you need inside you to Lead BOLDLY and Live FULLY.

With love, power, and purpose,

Anisa Rashad, MBA

Founder & CEO, ARE Global Solutions

Chapter One

The Frame

The photo frame on my desk has been there for years. A smiling family of four—me, Michael, the kids, and Lady, our little shih tzu—captured in the golden hour glow on a beach in The Bahamas. We looked radiant. Relaxed. Whole.

These days, I find myself staring at the frame more than at the people inside of it.

The woman in that photo…she looked so certain. So vibrant. So alive.

I barely recognize her anymore.

My Outlook calendar pinged. Another one-on-one. Another tense team conversation. Another moment to pretend I'm fine.

I closed my eyes and took a slow, deep breath—just like the therapist taught me. I haven't seen her in four months. Who has time for therapy when your team is underperforming, your home life is falling apart, and your boss—the Chief Human Resources Officer (CHRO) is subtly hinting that it might be time to "reevaluate your leadership approach"?

"Reevaluate what?" I muttered out loud.

I live in Clarksville, MD my dream zip code. I have my dream position as well, Vice President of People Strategy and Organizational Effectiveness at TriPoint Medical Center in Washington, DC. I'm not doing anything wrong. I'm just not doing anything that feels *right* anymore.

I reached for my coffee. Cold.

Just like my marriage has been for the last 18 months.

Just like my team's engagement scores.

Just like the space inside my chest every time Malik, my sixteen-year-old, closes his bedroom door without saying a word.

I glanced back at the photo again. It's not the job. Not entirely.

It's not Michael.

It's not even the kids.

It's the space between the Jil in that photo and the Jil sitting at this desk—surrounded by titles, bonuses, strategic plans, unread texts, and an emptiness I can't quite explain.

I used to feel alive in my work. Desired in my marriage. Connected—to my kids, to my body, to my purpose.

But now? Now I wake up already tired. I sit in meetings where my voice bounces back to me like an echo in an empty room. I come home to a house that's full—but I feel completely alone. I move through my days like an impeccably dressed ghost.

This morning, I knocked that picture frame off my desk while reaching for my phone. It landed face down, the corner chipped.

And for some reason…I didn't pick it up.

I just stared at it.

And then, without warning, a question rose up from somewhere deep inside me—one I hadn't dared to ask in years:

Is this what success is supposed to feel like?

Because if it is…I want a refund.

Chapter Two

The Beautiful Box

My office was pristine.

A white lacquered desk. Soft gray walls. Tasteful abstract art in muted tones. Not a single thing out of place. Even my pens were organized by color and function in the crystal holder I picked up during that leadership retreat in Sedona two years ago.

A retreat I barely remember.

Everything around me was beautiful. That's what I did, what I was known for. I made things beautiful. I made people feel beautiful. But somewhere along the way, something went wrong.

It's like the frame of my life doesn't match what it actually feels like to *live* this life.

My frame tells a perfect story: a good-looking, successful husband who just got promoted. Two healthy kids in private school. A beautiful home in a sought-after zip code. Luxury cars. Our sweet, spoiled shih tzu, Lady.

The woman inside that frame shouldn't feel invisible. Or empty. Or this alone.

I sat at my desk, watching my inbox fill like waves crashing on the shore. Meeting reminders. HR policy updates. One from our project lead:

Subject: Need to talk ASAP.

My stomach clenched.

Then came the buzz.

Michael.

Did you talk to Maya about the math grade yet? She said you promised.

I hadn't. I'd completely forgotten. Again.

A sharp bolt of guilt hit just beneath my ribs. I closed the message without replying.

Ping.

A calendar invite. Tracey—my boss—had scheduled a last-minute meeting.

Subject: Strategic Alignment Touchpoint

Time: 2:30 PM today.

My pulse quickened. I knew exactly what this was.

The feedback. The one she hinted at after the last all-hands. The one that sounded like:

"There's an opportunity for growth here…"

but felt more like,

"You're starting to look like a liability."

I glanced again at the woman in the frame. That smiling, glowing, golden-hour version of me.

She used to know who she was.

Now? I feel like a perfectly dressed stranger walking through the motions of my own life.

There was a knock. My assistant stepped in quietly.

"Hi, Jil. Sorry to interrupt. Tracey just confirmed she'll see you in the 9th-floor conference room."

I nodded, my throat tight. "Thanks, Tasha."

She paused. "You okay?"

I smiled. Soft. Practiced. "Always."

The door clicked shut.

I leaned back in my chair and exhaled slowly. There it was again— that soundless ache in my chest. Not quite panic. Not quite sadness.

Just the quiet grief of a woman who got everything she asked for… and still feels like something's missing.

Like I'd designed a beautiful box for myself and then somehow got locked inside it.

And inside that box, I feel small. Cramped. Like there's no room for the version of me that's curious, creative, messy, soft.

Some days, I don't know if I built the box myself…

Or if it was something I walked into.

Either way, I'm suffocating.

And no one knows.

That's the hardest part.

Because on the outside, it looks like I'm thriving. I have the salary. The team. The seat at the table. People look up to me. My team sends me birthday cakes and cards with hashtags like **#BossLady** and **#Superwoman**.

But no one knows I've been crying in the shower before work.

That I haven't touched my husband in months.

That I can't remember the last time I laughed from my belly—or felt proud of something I wasn't being paid to do.

I'm stuck.

And I'm scared to say it out loud.

Because what if saying it makes it real?

And if it's real…I don't know how to make it right.

I don't know how to get back to the old me—the one who smiled easily and meant it. The one who offered encouragement not just out of habit, but because she truly felt full enough to give it.

I'm not breaking down. Not exactly.

But I do feel that something needs to break open.

Chapter 3

The Assignment

The 9th floor was colder than usual.

Or maybe it was just me.

I walked the hallway slowly, my Brother Vellies pointy-toe pumps tapping a steady rhythm across the marble tile. I passed the familiar wall of glass-encased awards—Hospital Administration Leadership Recognition, Top 100 Women in Health, Best in Strategy Execution.

My name had been on one of them once. Three years ago.

Before the reorg.

Before Michael stopped smiling when I walked in the door.

Before Maya started slamming hers, and Malik stopped speaking in full sentences.

I reached the conference room and paused. Exhaled. Then opened the door.

Tracey was already seated—flawless as ever in a tailored navy blazer, a delicate gold necklace resting at her collarbone, lips soft and neutral, posture perfect. She smiled.

That CHRO smile. Warm. Measured. Direct.

"Jil, thanks for making time."

I slid into the seat across from her, crossing my legs like it was any other meeting. "Of course."

She folded her hands and leaned in ever so slightly. "I want to start by saying—we value you. I value you. You've made significant contributions, especially in the early integration phases."

Here it comes.

"But?" My stomach dropped. Tightened.

Was this a punishment?

A warning?

Was I failing and didn't know it yet?

She must've seen it in my face before I said a word.

"This isn't corrective," she said gently. "It's restorative."

I forced a smile, one I didn't feel. "Of course. I appreciate the support."

Tracey's smile deepened, but stayed soft. "Not a 'but.' A next step. One I believe you're ready for."

There it was again—that HR-coded language.

Framed like opportunity.

Delivered like a verdict.

"We've received some feedback," she continued. "Your team is competent. Capable. But disconnected. Performance metrics are holding… but morale is low. Engagement scores came back mixed."

My jaw clenched.

"And the truth is, Jil—you're too valuable to let that simmer. We want to invest in you. That's why we're assigning you an executive coach."

Assigning?

I blinked. "Assigning?"

Inside, I was screaming.

I don't need a coach.

I need sleep.

I need help.

I need someone—anyone—to understand how hard it is to lead when your soul is tired.

But I didn't say any of that.

I nodded.

Took the sleek white card she slid across the table.

Anisa Rashad, MBA
Founder & CEO, ARE Global Solutions
Visionary Connector | Strategic Leadership Architect

I stared at the embossed lettering. Heavy. Precise.

Tracey watched me, calm and direct. "I've been where you are. I know what it feels like to be surrounded by results… and still feel like something's not working."

She leaned in.

"Can I tell you something I've never shared with you?"

I nodded slowly. Unsure.

"I know you probably don't think you need this," she said. "I didn't either. But I've worked with Anisa personally. She's… different. She helped me through one of the hardest seasons of my life."

That got my attention.

Tracey? The woman who always seemed unshakeable.

"I don't talk about it much," she said quietly. "But a few years back, I was in a dark place. Quiet quitting, if I'm honest. I had the role, the recognition—but I was unraveling on the inside. My marriage was slipping. My confidence was shot. I felt like I was disappearing in plain sight."

My throat tightened.

That is me… me.

That is my *right now.*

"I started working with a coach," she said. "Reluctantly. But it turned out to be the turning point—not just in my career, but in my life."

She paused, her eyes soft with something that looked like reverence.

"Her name was Anisa. Anisa Rashad."

I sat up straighter. "That's who you are recommending for me? The same person you worked with?"

Tracey nodded. "Yes. She's the founder of ARE Global Solutions. A master coach and strategic leadership architect. She doesn't just coach leaders… she rebuilds them."

Jil let that land.

"I called her last week. Told her about you—not your name, but your situation. She said, 'I know her. I've seen her before. She's not broken. She's just out of alignment.'"

I swallowed hard.

"Anisa is very selective about who she works with, but she has agreed to meet with you. Said, *'If she shows up, I'll show up.'*"

Then she said the thing that broke me open just a little:

"Anisa helped me reclaim my voice. My rhythm. My vision. She reminded me that leadership doesn't have to leave you feeling depleted, alone, and unfulfilled—but, instead, can be a source of purpose, connection, and deep fulfillment."

I didn't say anything.

I just nodded.

Because what do you say when someone offers you a lifeline you didn't know how to ask for?

I left her office with the card in hand. Still unsure. Still guarded. Still convinced I didn't need anyone else poking around in my mess.

But something in her voice….

Something in the way she said *reclaim* kept echoing in my mind.

That night, I slid the card into my Telfar bag—the same one I bought when I first became VP. A gift to myself. A celebration of who I thought I was becoming.

Now it felt like I had just been handed a mirror… and an invitation.

And part of me was scared to look.

Chapter 4

The Encounter

I cried in the shower again this morning.

No big trigger. No big moment.

Just tears.

Again.

It was starting to feel like part of my morning routine.

By the time I got dressed and made it into the office lobby, the only thing louder than my heels on the tile was the alarm going off in my head: **Get coffee. Now.**

I detoured to Grounded Café, tucked in the corner of our building's first floor. A hidden gem that was no longer so hidden. The line was long. Of course it was.

I glanced at my watch. **8:15.**

I sighed. Opened my phone. Started scrolling.

My thumb hovered over Instagram.

I'd posted a picture of the kids last night—great lighting, matching outfits, even Lady was smiling.

62 likes.

One comment from a sorority sister I hadn't seen in two years:

"Sis, your family is beautiful! You're really doing it all!" #goals

I swallowed hard.

If only they knew.

As I adjusted my favorite Telfar tote—currently sagging with half my life inside—I heard a voice behind me. Warm. Grounded. Familiar in a way that made my spine straighten.

"You look like someone who's holding a lot… and doing a great job pretending it's not heavy."

I froze.

Who was this? How did she know?

I turned to see a woman smiling at me. Not smug. Not invasive. Just… knowing.

There was something about her energy—still, grounded, present. She didn't have to raise her voice to command space; her calm confidence, high vibration, and quiet magnetism simply drew you in.

Before I could talk myself out of it, I extended my hand and said,

"I'm Jil."

She shook it gently.

"Anisa. Anisa Rashad."

Wait—what?

My eyes widened.

The card. The coach.

This woman—the one I randomly bumped into in line for coffee—was the coach Tracey had insisted could help me find myself again?

I blinked. Took her in.

Coral jacket. Ivory silk blouse, denim slacks. gold hoops. Peep-toe pumps. Effortlessly chic.

She gave off *90210 CEO* with a side of *you-can-sit-with-me* energy.

Her presence didn't shout. It hummed.

And suddenly, everything connected.

Of course.

Of course it was her.

Anisa Rashad.

The name Tracey spoke with reverence.

The coach who helped her through her own unraveling.

The woman whose energy felt like clarity wrapped in calm.

I let out a soft, ironic laugh.

Not at her.

At life.

"Of course I would bump into *you* here. It's by divine order."

She smiled. Not surprised.

And just like that… something shifted.

Maybe having a coach wasn't a punishment after all.

Maybe Anisa wasn't just any coach—maybe she was *the* coach for me.

Maybe this meeting wasn't random. Maybe it was right on time.

And maybe—just maybe—this woman could help me find the Jil in that golden-hour photo in the Bahamas.

The one who knew joy.

The one who led with purpose.

The one who didn't just look whole…

She felt it.

The Decision

I sat at my desk, the coffee growing cold in my hand.

I didn't even remember what I ordered.

Anisa.

The name echoed in my head like a bell—low and persistent.

I hadn't said anything in that moment. I'd just nodded, thanked her for her words, took my coffee, and walked out. Like I had somewhere to be.

I did, but suddenly it didn't feel as urgent.

I opened my bag and pulled out the embossed card Tracey had given me.

Anisa Rashad, MBA

Founder and CEO of ARE Global Solutions

Visionary Connector. Strategic Leadership Architect.

How does someone radiate that kind of quiet freedom in the middle of a coffee line?

I stared at the number.

Then I did what any emotionally guarded, overperforming executive woman with control issues would do—I stared at it for twelve more minutes and thought of all the reasons not to call.

What if she wasn't available?

What if she was just… nice in public but one of those "surface coaches" who gives you worksheets and *TED Talk* quotes?

My finger hovered over the call button.

Then, almost without thinking, I hit another number.

Michael.

He picked up on the second ring. "Hey. Everything okay?"

I paused. "Yeah. I mean, yeah. I just wanted to… ask you something."

"That's new," he said, half-joking. "What's up?"

"I met someone today. A coach. Leadership. Life. All the things," I said, keeping my tone neutral. "Tracey gave me her contact information yesterday. We bumped into each other today in Grounded Café, and…I don't know, it felt like a sign."

There was silence on the line.

"I was thinking about calling her. Starting coaching. With everything going on… I think I need something."

"Another thing?" Michael said, his voice just barely sharp. "Jil, your calendar is already packed. Now you want to carve out more time—for *someone else*?"

"It's not someone else," I said, trying not to sound defensive. "It's me. I'm trying to get back to me."

More silence.

"I just…" he exhaled. "I get it, I do. But I'd be lying if I didn't say I feel like this is just one more way you're pulling away."

His words stung. Because there was some truth in them.

"I'm not pulling away," I said, softer now. "I'm trying to come back home to myself. And to us. But I need help getting there. Mike, I'm exhausted."

His voice dropped. "Then rest. You don't need a coach for that."

"Yes," I said. "I do. I need someone who sees me before I disappear completely."

He didn't respond right away. I waited, eyes stinging.

"Just promise me you won't forget about us while you're figuring it out," he finally said.

"I won't." My voice caught in my throat. "I can't."

I hung up before I changed my mind.

I stared at Anisa's number again.

And then I thought about what she said:

*"You look like someone who's holding a lot—and doing
a great job pretending it's not heavy."*

She saw me.

And it scared me how much I wanted someone to.

I took a deep breath.

Opened a new text.

Typed:

Hi Anisa. This is Jil Harrington. I believe we may have been divinely scheduled to work together. I'd like to schedule our first session. I believe I'm ready. Or at least I want to be.

My finger hovered over "send" for longer than I care to admit.

Then… I tapped it.

The message disappeared.

The silence in the office suddenly felt different. Not heavy—just quiet.

The kind of quiet right before something shifts.

Coaching Reflection

Session 0: The Moment Before the Moment

Jil hasn't officially started coaching—but the shift has already begun. This chapter captures her *pre-decision decision*: the sacred space between longing and action, fear and faith. Her call to Michael reflects the push-pull that so many high achievers face—the deep desire to grow and the fear that in doing so, they'll lose the people they love.

Anisa hasn't said much yet. But her presence—the way she *sees*— has already started peeling back layers.

This is the moment everything begins to change.

Anisa-ism™

"Sometimes the bravest thing you'll ever do is answer your own soul's whisper."

Inner Compass Check-In

This wasn't a coaching session. It was something deeper.

A threshold moment.

Jil didn't need a strategy yet—she needed stillness. Space. And permission to choose herself.

Take a breath with her.

- Where in your life are you hovering over the "send" button?
- What would shift if you stopped overthinking and trusted your own readiness?
- What might open if you allowed one small, sacred "yes" to be enough for today?

You don't have to map the whole path.

You just have to move toward the part of you that's already waiting to break open.

Chapter 5

Believe BOLDLY – The First Session

I arrived fifteen minutes early. That's how I do anxiety—early, overprepared, and in full makeup.

The office was tucked inside a co-working space downtown—exposed brick, natural light, soft jazz playing low in the background. It didn't feel corporate. It felt… calm. Human. Intentional.

Anisa's assistant greeted me warmly and offered herbal tea. I passed. The way my nerves and bladder were set up, I didn't need more liquid.

When I walked into the coaching room, Anisa stood and extended her hand. "Welcome, Jil."

I shook her hand. Firm, professional. I knew how to play this game.

She motioned to the chair across from her. No desk between us. Just two comfy chairs and a small table with a pitcher of water, a candle, a Zen desktop garden, and what looked like a small stack of cards.

I sat down. Smoothed my pants. Crossed my legs. Waited.

Anisa didn't rush. She sat across from me, grounded. Centered. Like she had all the time in the world.

"Before we start," she said gently, "I want to be clear: This space isn't about fixing you. You're not broken. We're just here to listen for the parts of you that may have gone quiet—and invite them back."

I blinked. No one had ever opened a meeting like that with me before.

She continued. "You have nothing to hide, nothing to defend, nothing to protect, and nothing to prove."

And then she asked, "What would you like to walk away with at the end of our time together?"

I froze. My mind scanned for the right answer, the professional answer, the "I've read a thousand books on leadership" answer.

But what came out was: "Honestly? I'm here because my boss told me to be."

Anisa smiled. "Fair."

I shifted. "But also… because I'm tired. And not just tired. Disconnected. From my team. My family. Myself. I want to feel like myself again."

She nodded slowly. "That's a powerful intention."

We started with the basics—what she called the 4A Coaching Model: Awareness, Analysis, Action, and Achievement. We were in the *Awareness* phase.

She asked questions that no one had ever asked me before. Not my boss. Not my therapist. Not even my husband.

"Where in your life do you feel most out of alignment?" "What have you learned to tolerate that is no longer sustainable?" "When was the last time you felt fully seen—at work or at home?"

I didn't have answers.

But the questions unlocked something.

She asked me to share the voices in my head when I wake up each morning. I laughed, then cried.

She then stated with the most compassion I've ever felt: "What if your exhaustion isn't a flaw in your system but a signal from your soul?"

I just sat there blinking rapidly. My eyes stung. Not because it was dramatic—but because it was true.

"Let's talk about what it means to *Believe BOLDLY*," Anisa said, leaning in slightly. "It means choosing belief over fear. It means trusting yourself in rooms where you were told to shrink. It means remembering your voice when everyone else is speaking louder. And sometimes it just means saying 'I am enough'—out loud, without apology."

I swallowed. Something about that struck me deep.

"Can I tell you a story?" I asked.

She nodded.

"A few years ago, we were finalizing a merger with a neighboring hospital—a historic move for the medical center that would expand our reach and reshape healthcare delivery in our region. The chief strategy officer fell ill the night before the final negotiation meeting. I was asked to step in. No prep, just instinct. I walked into that boardroom filled with CEOs, board members, and legal teams—and I led with clarity and conviction. Not forcefully, but fully. I believed in our vision. I believed in the future we were building. And they said yes. That agreement didn't just change our institution's trajectory—it changed the course of my career."

Anisa smiled. "That's the woman we're inviting back."

"Each week, you'll get a simple but powerful truth—part wisdom, part encouragement—designed to anchor you in who you are and what's possible. Over time, my clients began calling them "Anisa-isms," small but mighty phrases they would request at the end of our sessions to carry them through the week. What started as spontaneous moments of inspiration have now become a signature part of the Lead BOLDLY Live FULLY™ journey—guiding leaders back to their power, their purpose, and themselves.

She handed me a card. I read it out loud. "You don't have to lose yourself to lead others."

I held it in my hands like a permission slip. Like a prayer.

Later that afternoon

I drove to Rock Creek park. Between the water, the massive oaks, and the walking trails it always makes me feel grounded. I parked. Opened my notebook that was filled with all my work obligations. Stared at the page.

And then I began to write.

Dear Me, I miss you.

You used to take up space without apology. You laughed loudly. You trusted your gut. You were brilliant—not just in outcome, but in energy. You connected. You created. You made people feel seen. Including me.

Somewhere along the way, I got consumed with titles, deadlines, and responsibilities. I kept achieving, but I stopped celebrating. I kept giving, but I stopped feeling. And now… I want you back.

Not just the boldness. The *belief.*

I want to remember what it feels like to walk into a room and know I belong. To know I don't have to lose myself to lead others.

Love, Jil

I closed the notebook. Exhaled slowly. For the first time in a long time, the tears that rolled down my face weren't from burnout. They were from release.

Something had *shifted.*

Coaching Reflection

In this foundational session, Jil entered the *Awareness* phase of the 4A Coaching Model. Through grounding questions and intentional space, she uncovered her core intention: reconnection—with her work, her family, and herself. Anisa introduced the theme for this chapter: Believe BOLDLY, the first pillar of the BOLD Leadership Framework. Belief is the foundation of everything—and Jil is just beginning to reclaim hers.

Anisa-ism™

"You don't have to lose yourself to lead others."

Inner Compass Check-In

- Where in your life have you been performing instead of belonging?
- What are you tired of hiding or proving?
- Who is the version of you that still believes? What would it take to bring her back?

Write her a letter. Welcome her home.

Growth Assignment

Write a letter to the version of yourself who believes boldly. Speak to her like a friend. A guide. A future you. Let her remind you of what you've forgotten.

Optional bonus: Read your letter aloud to yourself in the mirror. Let the words land.

Chapter 6

Organize Strategically

I stared at the screen, blinking. My calendar looked like a patchwork quilt of meetings I didn't remember accepting. One-on-ones. Strategic planning. A leadership team check-in I wasn't really contributing to. And somehow, two overlapping invites labeled "Mandatory."

I sat in Anisa's office, laptop open, judgment thick in my own throat.

"How do I look at this every day," I muttered, "and still pretend I'm in control?"

Anisa sat across from me, calm and composed. I could tell she wasn't there to fix my schedule—she was here to help me see what it was really saying.

"Your calendar," she said, "isn't just a time management tool. It's a values map."

I looked at her, confused.

She continued. "It shows what you're prioritizing—whether you mean to or not. And when your time is out of alignment with your values… burnout becomes your baseline."

I stared at the blocks of time on the screen again. None of it felt like mine.

"Do you know the last time I blocked out space for strategy?" I asked.

She didn't answer.

"Me neither."

"What do you wish your calendar said about you?" she asked softly.

That stopped me. What a question.

I looked down again. I saw meetings, deadlines, deliverables, everyone else's needs. But where was the leadership development I used to love? The team connection time I said I valued? The space to think, not just react?

It hit me. My calendar was a reflection of my coping. Not my calling.

She slid a card across the table—another Anisa-ism, packed with gut-punching intention:

"Don't just manage your time—honor it."

Then she smiled and said, "Let's look at your calendar again. This time, like a map—not a minefield."

Anisa slid another sheet across the table. At the top it read:

Calendar Values Map

"Here's the truth," she said gently. "Your calendar is already telling a story. The question is—does it tell your story, or everyone else's?"

She asked me to write down my top five values. The ones I said mattered most to me.

I stared at the page for a moment, then wrote:

- Growth
- Family
- Creativity
- Leadership
- Connection

"Good," she nodded. "Now, let's test them."

She printed out the last two weeks of my calendar and handed me a pack of highlighters.

"Green means it clearly reflects your values," she explained. "Yellow if it somewhat aligns. Red if it doesn't align at all."

I went line by line. Meeting after meeting.

Green was rare.

Yellow showed up here and there.

But red bled across the page like an alarm I'd been ignoring.

My throat tightened.

"This is my life," I whispered. "But it doesn't look like me."

Anisa leaned forward. "That's because you've been performing instead of prioritizing. This exercise isn't about judgment—it's about clarity. Now you know the gap. And gaps can be closed."

She placed a fresh calendar page in front of me.

"Your turn. Rewrite next week. This time, every value gets a place."

We pulled out the colored Post-its—purple for personal restoration, yellow for family time, blue for deep work, and green for creative space. Piece by piece, the puzzle came together.

It wasn't perfect. But for the first time in months, my week looked like a reflection of who I said I wanted to be.

She introduced me to a new concept: Becoming a TEAM—a Time, Energy, and Attention Manager.

"You don't just need a better planner," she said. "You need a better philosophy."

That was the shift. She didn't just help me reorganize my week. She helped me reimagine what deserved space in my life.

We laughed. We played. We moved things around like puzzle pieces. She asked me to put myself on the calendar first. A workout. A solo lunch. Time with my daughter. Creative hours.

"It's not about the goal—it's the daily practice," she said.

That line? That's the one I wrote on my bathroom mirror. That's the one I texted to Leah when she said she was struggling to juggle work and the preparation for being a new mom. That's the one I whispered when I got home, opened my laptop, and started canceling things that didn't belong in the life I'm reconstructing.

It wasn't perfect. But it was progress. And that's where transformation begins.

Coaching Reflection

This session focused on helping Jil shift from a time-starved executive trapped by her calendar to an intentional leader who could see it as a values map. Anisa introduced the concept of *Organize Strategically*—the second pillar of the BOLD Leadership Framework—and guided Jil through a Calendar Values Alignment exercise. Instead of scheduling for performance, Jil began redesigning her time around what mattered most, learning to manage not just hours but her time, energy, and attention.

Anisa-ism™

"When your time is out of alignment with your values, burnout becomes your baseline."

Inner Compass Check-In

- Where does your calendar reflect your calling — and where does it reflect your coping?
- Which of your core values show up in your schedule — and which ones have you quietly abandoned?
- If someone looked at your last two weeks, what story would your calendar tell about you?
- What truth is your calendar telling you that you've been avoiding?
- How would it feel to put yourself on the calendar first — and who might you become if you did?

Growth Assignment

- Identify your top 3–5 values — the ones you say matter most.
- Print or pull up your last two weeks of calendar activity.

- Highlight each item: **Green** if it reflects your values, **Yellow** if it somewhat aligns, **Red** if it doesn't align at all.
- Tally the results. What's your alignment ratio?
- Now create your **Calendar Values Map**: redesign the coming week so that every value has a visible place. Use colors, blocks of time, or Post-its to make it tangible.
- Choose one value that's been missing and protect that time like it matters — because it does.

Optional bonus: Share your Calendar Values Map with a trusted colleague, mentor, or friend. Accountability is love

Chapter 7

Lead with Intention

Anisa didn't start this session with strategy. She started with silence.

"Close your eyes," she said. "I want you to visualize a day where you feel aligned—where your presence is your power."

I did. And what I saw wasn't a boardroom or a podium. It was my kitchen. Laughing with Maya. Sitting next to Michael without tension in the air. Walking into a meeting and not pretending.

When I opened my eyes, she was smiling. "That's the version of you we're building toward."

She passed me another card from the LBLF Activation Set. This one had a gold foil sunburst in the corner. It read:

"Being present is a gift—to yourself and to the people you lead."

I read it twice.

"This one's going in my purse," I said quietly.

She nodded. "I designed those cards to remind my clients that their power isn't in what they produce—it's in how they show up."

A QR code was printed on the back. "You can grab a full set online," she added. "They're a practice in your pocket."

We got into the real work—leading from a centered place instead of defaulting to performance.

"You've been leading from duty," Anisa said. "Let's help you lead from desire."

She invited me to rewrite my leadership narrative. Not the resume version. The real one.

What did I want to be known for? How did I want people to feel in my presence?

"It's not about the role," she said. "It's about the ripple."

That one made me pause. It made me think of Tracey—how she led with warmth and truth, how she had changed the entire tone of our People & Culture team. How she had left ripples in rooms she no longer even walked into.

And for the first time in a long time, I thought: Maybe I could be that kind of leader, too.

At the end of the session, Anisa smiled and slid the card back toward me. "Let it be more than a quote," she said. "Let it be a way of being."

Two weeks into coaching, and I was already noticing things I used to ignore: how my shoulders crept up to my ears during meetings… how I held my breath when someone said, "Can I give you some feedback?"… how I filled silences because I didn't want to sit with discomfort.

This morning, I'd made a decision: I wasn't going to sprint through the day. I was going to *lead* it.

Anisa had called it "anchoring your leadership in intention." She said intention wasn't just about what you do—it's about *who you're being* while you do it.

My first test came at 9 a.m. on Wednesday, at the weekly staff meeting with my People Strategy and Organizational Effectiveness team at TriPoint Medical Center. The usual suspects: status updates, shallow wins, unspoken tension.

I walked in a few minutes early, laptop in hand, and greeted my team one by one. I noticed Priya was unusually quiet, and Nia's eyes looked tired.

Normally, I would've launched into the agenda, checked the clock, and moved us along.

But I paused. Took a breath.

I opened the meeting with one question:

"What's one thing that's getting in the way of your best work right now?"

The room went still.

For a second, I thought I'd lost them.

Then Joon, my most reserved team lead, looked up and said, "Honestly? I'm afraid to ask for help because I don't want to seem like I can't handle it."

And just like that… the air changed.

People leaned in. Real conversation unfolded. Priya shared that she was covering for two people and barely sleeping. Nia admitted she was considering leaving the team. And instead of reacting with performance-Jil—defensive, overwhelmed, controlling—I paused.

I remembered what Anisa said: *Being present is a gift to you and the team you lead.*

I thanked them. I asked questions. I didn't worry about next week or tomorrow or try fix everything. I showed up differently, now, in the present moment.

And they did, too.

After the meeting, I texted Anisa:

> **Me:** Tried something different in staff. One question opened the door.
>
> **Anisa:** That's what intention does. It clears space for honesty—and impact.

Later that day, I had a one-on-one with Tracey, my boss. I didn't lead with updates or metrics. I led with clarity.

"I want to be transparent about how I'm evolving," I said. "I'm looking at how I've led in the past and choosing to be more intentional moving forward. I'm not here to perform—I'm here to lead with intention."

She looked up. Surprised.

Then… she smiled.

"That's exactly the Jil I knew was still in there."

Back in my office, I opened the blank calendar Anisa had given me. I started filling it in—not with tasks, but with intention.

- Focus time for thinking, not just doing.

- 15-minute blocks between back-to-back meetings to breathe and reset
- Time to connect—not just correct—with my team.

It wasn't perfect. But for the first time in a long time, my calendar felt like a reflection of me, my values. A could feel something rising inside of me. What was it? Was that perhaps a spark of joy?

Coaching Reflection

In this session, Anisa guided Jil into the third pillar of the BOLD Leadership Framework: *Lead with Intention*. Through visualization, reflection, and real-time leadership moments, Jil began showing up, not just as an executor—but as a catalyst. She is learning that leadership isn't just about getting results. It's about creating *ripples* that outlast you.

Anisa-ism™

"Being present is a gift—to yourself and to the people you lead."

Inner Compass Check-In

- What kind of ripple do you want to leave in every room you enter?
- Where have you been leading from performance instead of being truly present?
- How would your team describe you on your best day? Your worst?

Growth Assignment

- Identify one recurring meeting you lead.
- Choose one intention to bring into that space this week (ex., curiosity, patience, authenticity).
- Reflect on the difference it makes—in energy, tone, and outcomes.

Optional bonus: Invite your team to co-create the intention with you. Watch what shifts.

Chapter 8

Drive Results

Jil stepped into the serene coaching suite like she was stepping onto a runway—intentional, composed, yet carrying the quiet weight of a thousand unspoken thoughts. Her outfit was a masterclass in elegance with edge: a tailored, double-breasted blazer dress in deep emerald green cinched perfectly at the waist with a statement belt. Clothes had always been her armor. As she took her seat in the comfy chair next to Anisa, she felt strong yet vulnerable.

As if reading my unspoken thoughts, Anisa handed me a new card and said, "You were never the problem,"

This one read:

"It's not about the output. It's about the alignment."

That one made me sit up straighter.

Because results had always been my currency. I delivered. I overdelivered. And I did it at the expense of myself, over and over again.

So when Anisa invited me to look at my last performance review, I braced myself. It was good—on paper. But we both knew something was missing.

"Let's redefine what results mean to you, not just to them," she said.

We began to map my goals through a new lens—not just quarterly KPIs, but with clarity, integrity, joy, and boundaries.

Anisa called the process *Results Redefinition.*

"You were hired to produce," she said. "But you were born to lead."

Another Anisa-ism card slid across the table:

"Burnout is not a badge of honor."

It hit me harder than I expected.

We moved through my upcoming goals: one high-stakes presentation, a key hire, and a strategic offsite.

"Which of these are performance-driven?" she asked. "And which are purpose-driven?"

The room got quiet.

We designed new ways to approach each goal with less stress and more clarity. More collaboration. More coaching instead of carrying.

I started assigning, not absorbing.

At the end of our session, Anisa handed me a page from the **Lead BOLDLY. Live FULLY™ Planner**.

She smiled, sliding it across the table like she was handing me something sacred.

"Jil, you don't just need a better planner. You need a better philosophy. The **Lead BOLDLY. Live FULLY™ Planner** helps you create **values-based results with strategy, sustainability, and significance**. It's the blueprint for impact without exhaustion."

She leaned in slightly. "I created the planner to help leaders keep their results aligned with their values—not just what they check off, but how they show up."

I glanced down at the page in front of me, realizing I wasn't just holding a new tool.

"I was holding the key to leading my life with purpose—and without exhaustion."

Another QR code, another tool to take home.

By the time I left, I didn't just have a to-do list. I had a blueprint—for impact without exhaustion.

And I believed for the first time in years: I could lead and still have something left for myself.

Two days later, I sat in the small conference room off the Innovation Wing with Leah Cohen.

She was one of the brightest individuals I'd ever mentored—quick, thoughtful, and tenacious.

Leah is 33, married to her college sweetheart, and five months pregnant with their first child. She's an engineering manager at Innovative Engineering Solutions, a firm we partnered with for all major medical equipment renovations at TriPoint Medical Center.

Over the past year, she'd been stepping into a bigger role, fielding more client-facing projects and internal initiatives. There have been whispers that she is in line for the Director of Systems Integration once it opens up after the restructure.

And if I were honest, she'd earned it.

But I could also see the weight she was carrying.

She sat across from me, glowing but tired, her water bottle at the ready and a notebook full of project notes.

"Thank you for making time," she said. "I've been trying to balance excitement about maternity leave with the anxiety that I'm stepping back at the wrong time."

I nodded. "That tension is real. You're not alone in that."

She gave a half-laugh. "I just don't want anyone to forget what I've built. I've worked too hard for too long to lose momentum."

I could see pieces of my former self in her. The over-functioning. The proving. The pressure.

And just for a moment, I almost responded the way I used to. With strategy. With a checklist. With advice that sounded helpful—but was really just more noise.

Instead, I paused. Breathed.

"Leah," I said gently. "Do you want a tool that helped me realign how I define results?"

She nodded quickly. "Please."

I handed her a Results Redefinition worksheet—the blank one Anisa had given me to use later.

"We're taught to deliver outcomes, but we're not taught to measure how those outcomes feel—or what they cost us."

We worked through it together. Her goal to finalize the MRI suite reconfiguration was clear. But we added new dimensions: How do you want to feel when it's done? What boundaries do you need to honor? What kind of support would make this sustainable?"

By the end, she was writing with purpose.

"I needed this," she whispered. "I didn't know how much."

Later that day, I had a 1:1 with Tracey.

We met in her office, where a diffuser was humming and her shelves were full of books that always made me want to read more—and lead better.

"How's the coaching going?" she asked, looking up with that piercing but kind gaze.

"I'm a different leader than I was eight weeks ago," I said. "Not because I've added anything. But because I've *let go* of so much."

Tracey smiled. "That's real leadership. And it shows. Your team sees it. And I see it, too."

We talked about my upcoming offsite, and I told her I was co-designing with Anisa's ARE Global Solutions team and members of my team this time. "Intention over control," I said.

She nodded slowly. "You're not just leading better. You're leading *boldly*."

When Michael stepped into the house that evening, the familiar scent of simmering lentils and rosemary met him at the door. Briefcase in hand, he loosened his tie with one hand and paused—just long enough to take her in before she noticed him.

There she was—standing at the stove, soft music playing low in the background, swaying ever so slightly as she stirred. Nothing dramatic. Nothing loud. But something was different.

Lighter. That was the word that came to him.

She didn't look like someone carrying the weight of ten competing meetings or the exhaustion of trying to hold everyone else together. Not tonight. Her shoulders weren't hunched. Her jaw wasn't clenched. And there was something about the way she was singing—off key, yes, but still—it had been a long time since he'd heard that sound.

He watched for another beat, quietly assessing her without wanting her to know. He'd learned to read her over the years—not just what she said, but what she didn't. And lately, there'd been subtle signs: the return of soft candles on the mantle, jazz playlists while she worked, earrings she hadn't worn in months showing up in the rotation again. The callouses around her joy were starting to thin.

She was turning a corner.

He could see it in her face. Something at work had shifted. Something inside her too. She seemed more grounded, more sure. And yet He couldn't ignore that while she seemed to be reclaiming pieces of herself, she hadn't quite turned toward *him*. Their rhythm at home still felt off—like two people dancing to different songs. Peaceful, yes. Respectful. But distant.

They hadn't fought in a while, which on the surface felt like progress. But deep down, he knew it was just silence not resolution.

Still, he felt the shift. And it softened something in him, too.

He walked up behind her, pressed a gentle kiss to her cheek, and said quietly, "You seem lighter."

She smiled. Just slightly.

And in that small, flickering moment, he wondered if the light she was finding might one day find its way back to them.

She smiled. "I'm trying."

But the next moment reminded Jil she still had work to do.

Maya came downstairs in tears—barefoot, hoodie sleeves pulled over her hands, eyes red and brimming. She clutched her phone like it was both weapon and wound.

"What's wrong?" Jil asked, "It's stupid," Maya sniffled, though her trembling voice betrayed how *not* stupid it felt. "The group chat… they were saying things. About me. About my hair. About… everything."

Before she could finish, I was already on my feet.

"What did they say? Let me see." I held out my hand, all business.

Maya hesitated. Her body tensed, shoulders rising like a drawbridge. *Here she goes again*, her eyes seemed to say.

I was in full Jil-fix-it mode. Efficient. Commanding. Intent on crafting the perfect message to shut it all down and teach a lesson while I was at it. I was two swipes away from texting thirteen-year-olds like a PR crisis manager.

Michael stepped in quietly and laid a hand on my arm, just enough pressure to interrupt the autopilot.

"Maybe she doesn't need answers," he said softly. "Maybe she just needs you to sit with her."

His words pierced through the noise in my head like sunlight through blinds.

I looked at Maya again, really looked. Her fists were clenched around her hoodie sleeves. Her jaw was tight. And yet, her eyes were pleading. Not for a solution. For a soft place to land.

She didn't want a fixer. She wanted a mother.

I let out a slow breath, lowered my hand, and walked over to the couch. "Come here, baby."

She hesitated, surprised.

But then she came, curling beside me like she used to when she was little. I didn't ask another question. Didn't offer a plan. Just wrapped my arm around her and let her talk. No interruptions. No advice. Just presence.

Maya leaned her head on my shoulder. *This*, she thought. *This is the mom I wish I could see more of.* Not the executive. Not the enforcer. Just… her.

Michael stood a few feet away, watching the two of us quietly. There was something unspoken in the room, something fragile and sacred.

I was growing.

But I wasn't done yet.

Coaching Reflection

In this final BOLD coaching session, Anisa introduced the fourth pillar of the framework: *Drive Results*—not from depletion, but from alignment. Jil learned to reframe success beyond productivity and to measure impact through strategy, sustainability, and significance. Now she was ready to start working on showing up this way more consistently at home.

Anisa-ism™

"It's not about the output. It's about the alignment."

Inner Compass Check-In

- What results are you chasing that no longer align with who you are becoming?
- What would it look like to measure your success in terms of presence, clarity, and impact—not just productivity?
- Who is someone you can mentor using what you're learning?

Growth Assignment

- Complete your own *Results Redefinition* worksheet.
- Choose one upcoming goal or deliverable and ask:
- How do I want to feel when this is complete?
- What boundaries must I honor?
- Who can support me?

Optional bonus: Share this framework with someone you lead or mentor. See what it unlocks.

Chapter 9

From Leading Boldly to Living Fully

Today was all about reflection. The final BOLD coaching session had ended quietly.

No fanfare. No recap presentation. Just me, sitting across from Anisa, breathing a little deeper than I did eight weeks ago.

"Feels different, doesn't it?" she said.

I nodded. "I thought transformation would feel bigger. Louder."

She smiled. "It's often quiet. But it's something you can refer back to for a lifetime."

There was something sacred in the stillness. Like the ground beneath me had settled. My calendar had changed. My language had changed. My posture—literally and figuratively—had changed.

But more than anything, my **relationship with myself** had changed.

I was no longer performing leadership. I was practicing it.

And yet…

"I'm proud of the progress," I said. "But if I'm honest, there's still something missing."

Anisa leaned forward. "Tell me more."

"I'm showing up better at work. My team feels the shift. I feel it. But when the laptop closes… when I go home and it's just me and Michael, or Malik or Maya, or the stillness of a quiet house—I still feel unanchored. Like I'm doing everything *better*, but not necessarily feeling *more full*."

Anisa didn't look surprised. She just nodded. As if she'd been waiting for this moment.

"That's because BOLD is about **how** you lead," she said. "But LIFE is about **why** you live."

I sat back.

"LIFE?"

Yes, LIFE. Anisa said slowly, "The LIFE Fulfillment Framework, A Foundation for Sustainable Success" came after The BOLD Leadership Framework. I created it because I realized many of my clients were leading incredibly well—but living deeply unfulfilled."

She turned one of the cards over. The word *Fulfillment* glowed beneath a sunburst.

"I remember coaching a hospital CEO years ago," she said. "He had restructured a broken system, built pipelines of talent, and was beloved by his board. But his health was failing. His marriage was hanging on by a shoestring. His relationship with his children was barely existent and his laugh—gone. He had done everything 'right' professionally. But he wasn't living."

Anisa looked at me with such clarity, I felt seen all over again.

"Leadership without fulfillment isn't sustainable," she said. "That's why I built the LIFE Fulfillment Framework. Because I don't want to help people perform better in systems that are draining the life out of them. I want to help them create lives—and legacies—they actually *want* to live."

I felt that.

In my bones.

"So what now?" I asked.

She slid a new card across the table.

"You get to live a life you don't need a vacation from."

Anisa stood up and motioned for me to follow her to the whiteboard.

"We'll walk through each of the LIFE pillars together," she said. "But not today. You've done deep reflective work today. We honor that."

She turned to face me.

"Before we move into LIFE, I want you to name what's still calling to you. What's still unsatisfied?"

I took a deep breath.

"I want to reconnect to joy. I want more laughter in my life. More creativity. I want to feel energized by my days, not just proud of them."

She nodded. "That's where we begin."

She handed me a soft, coral-colored journal. On the front it read: *Live Inspired Fully Every Day.*

"Take this," she said. "Write freely. Not for productivity. Not for reflection. Just expression. Let yourself hear yourself."

I held it like it was sacred.

And maybe it was.

Coaching Reflection

This transition session marked the close of Jil's BOLD Leadership Framework journey and opened the door to the LIFE Fulfillment Framework. Anisa shared the origin and purpose of the LIFE model, rooted in sustainable, whole-life transformation. Jil identified lingering disconnection beyond her professional growth and began preparing to explore joy, creativity, and deeper alignment in her personal life.

Anisa-ism™

"You get to live a life you don't need a vacation from."

Inner Compass Check-In

- What areas of your life feel successful but not fulfilling?
- Where are you still going through the motions?
- What would it look like to live inspired—fully, not just occasionally?

Growth Assignment

- Begin journaling in your LIFE journal. Not for work. Not for goals. Just for you.

- Write freely about what inspires you, what you miss, what lights you up.

- Reflect on the gap between achievement and fulfillment in your life—and prepare to close it.

Chapter 10

Live on Purpose

It wasn't a dramatic moment. It was a Tuesday. Not a retreat. Not a birthday. Just a regular morning in Clarksville—gray skies, lukewarm coffee, Maya humming in the kitchen, and me, standing in front of my closet, realizing something had changed.

For years, I had chosen my clothes based on the roles I needed to play. The VP. The fixer. The mom who didn't cry in the car line. But today, I asked a new question: "What would the real me wear today?"

And that question spilled over into everything. What would the real me eat for breakfast? What meetings would the real me cancel—or walk into with boldness? What conversations would I stop avoiding?

This was the beginning of living on purpose.

Anisa had been preparing me for it. She handed me a card weeks ago that I had stuck on the dashboard of my car. It read: "You don't find your purpose. You live it—one decision at a time."

That morning, I finally understood it. I didn't need a five-year plan. I needed five minutes of truth.

Later that day, I made two small shifts: I called my team lead and delegated a project I'd been micromanaging for months. And I texted Michael: Let's talk tonight. Just us. No kids. No drama.

He didn't reply right away. I saw the three dots appear… and disappear. But that evening he came home with takeout from our favorite Thai spot, the one we used to go to before life got so busy.

We sat on the back porch looking out at the tall trees, feeling the warm breeze cutting through the evening stillness. I love trees, it's the reason I wanted to live in Clarksville. I wanted to be away from the hustle and bustle of the city.

The kids were inside, the house unusually quiet. For a few minutes, we ate in silence—side by side, but not quite together. He was on one end of our Loveseat Swing. I was on the other. Our feet didn't touch. But our energy did. Tentative. Tense. Tender.

He kept glancing at me—almost like he was trying to read a version of me he didn't quite recognize yet. And honestly, I wasn't sure I recognized her either.

Finally, I broke the silence.

"I don't want to perform anymore," I said. "Not in my career. Not in this marriage."

I expected a snarky remark. Sarcasm. Something. But instead, he looked at me, really looked and nodded.

"Me either," he said quietly.

We didn't reach for each other. There were no grand declarations. But in that moment, something softened. A layer of armor we'd both been carrying for too long cracked, just enough to let a little light in.

It wasn't a fix. We still had miles to go.

But it was the first time in a long time we sat together without pretending.

And that felt like a beginning

Living on purpose didn't mean I had all the answers. It meant I was finally asking the right questions.

At my next coaching session, Anisa smiled before I even sat down. "You look different," she said. "I feel different."

She slid me a new card. This one I keep in my wallet: "You don't need a new life. You need a new lens."

Every time I pulled it out, I remembered: This wasn't a pivot. This was a homecoming.

It started with a candle. A simple white one in a glass jar with the smell of lavender and jasmine. Sitting still, I lit it the morning after one of my coaching sessions with Anisa—the one where she asked me:

"What parts of your life are happening to you… and what parts are happening through you?"

I didn't have an answer. So I lit the candle. Sat on the edge of my bed. And just… breathed. No phone. No music. No email. Just me and a flicker of light in a quiet house before the world remembered I existed.

That moment changed something. It wasn't monumental, but it was mine. And it felt like purpose. Not a job title. Not a goal. Just presence.

Anisa had said: "Living on purpose doesn't mean having a five-year plan. It means showing up for your life like it matters. Because it does." So I started making small decisions like I believed that.

I set my phone to Do Not Disturb from 9:30 a.m. to 10:30 a.m.—an hour just for deep work. I blocked time to have lunch with Maya at her favorite salad spot after school—no laptop, no excuses. I let Malik ride in the car without me peppering him with questions. We just rode. In silence. Together.

Presence is a form of leadership too.

For the first time in months, I took a walk during the golden hour. Just me and Lady, my little shih tzu, prancing down the sidewalk like we had nowhere to be. And in that golden light, I caught a reflection of us in a neighbor's window. I didn't look accomplished. I didn't look like a VP. I didn't look like I had it all together. I looked present. And somehow, that was enough.

I texted Anisa later that night: Me: I think I'm learning how to live again. On purpose. Anisa: That's how it starts. One moment of truth at a time.

The next morning, I arrived early to the office—not to get a head start, but to breathe. I sat in my car, journal in hand, and reread some of the things I had written for a few minutes before walking in. There, in that parking garage, I began a ritual. I called it my Purpose Pause. Just five minutes to ask: What would it look like to lead on purpose today?

Some days, the answer was clear—speak up in the meeting, push back on unrealistic timelines, or call a colleague just to say thank you. Other days, it was simply: Don't hide. Be seen.

The more I honored these nudges, the more aligned my life felt. I was still busy, still leading, still managing deadlines. But the frantic striving had softened. I wasn't trying to *be* anything. I was just learning to *be*—and lead—from a place of truth.

One afternoon, Leah popped into my office. She's an engineering manager at Innovative Engineering Solutions and my mentee. brilliant, sometimes overly eager, always deeply curious with a strong faith. "Can I ask you something?" she said.

"Always."

"How do you know when you're living on purpose?"

I paused, then smiled. "You just asked the right question."

I shared my journal story. The dashboard quote. The deep breaths. The silent car rides. She listened intently, then said: "I've been trying to force clarity. Maybe I need to create space for it."

"Yes," I said. "Purpose doesn't shout. It whispers. And you have to be quiet enough to hear it."

She nodded slowly. "So it's not about finding my purpose. It's about aligning with it?"

I smiled again. "Exactly."

We continued our conversation, and she left with her usual bounce, plus the gentle sway that comes with being this close to her due date. Watching her, I remembered my own final days of pregnancy — the mix of anticipation and exhaustion, the way every step felt like carrying both a burden and a miracle. In a way, that's where I found myself too: swollen with questions I could no longer ignore, carrying the weight of change I hadn't yet birthed. Like Leah, I was on the edge of something new, even if I couldn't fully name it yet."

That night, Michael surprised me with a picnic at the same park where we used to go before the kids were born. No big gestures—just a blanket, a couple of takeout containers, and the kind of quiet that doesn't need filling.

We didn't say much. Just watched the sun dip low behind the trees, shadows stretching long across the grass.

Then, without a word, he reached for my hand.

"You feel more like you lately," he said softly, his thumb brushing over mine.

"I am," I whispered. "Not because life is easier. But because I finally stopped pretending it should be."

He nodded—no fanfare, no fix-it energy. Just presence. Gentle and grounding.

After a while, we packed up in silence, drove home with the windows down, and moved through the house like we'd finally exhaled something we didn't know we'd been holding.

Later, once the kids were settled and the dishwasher hummed in the background, I slipped into our bedroom. Michael had already gone to shower, the sound of water soft behind the door. I sat on the edge of the bed for a moment, the night still wrapped around me like a warm shawl.

That's when I saw the new card from my coaching session, resting on the nightstand where I'd left it.

"Living on purpose isn't about what you do—it's about
how fully you show up in the doing."

I placed it beside the candle and watched the flame flicker gently, steady and alive.

Maybe this, too, was purpose—not a grand epiphany, but a quiet return to self. And maybe I wasn't doing it alone.

I didn't need to chase clarity.

I just needed to choose presence.

And day by day, moment by moment, that's exactly what I was learning to do.

The card for this week's coaching session was "Living on purpose isn't about what you do—it's about how fully you show up in the doing."

I placed it on my nightstand, next to the candle. A reminder: I didn't need to chase clarity. I needed to choose presence.

And day by day, moment by moment, that's exactly what I did.

Coaching Reflection:

In this powerful first pillar of the **LIFE Fulfillment Framework™**, we find Jil making meaningful strides—quickly incorporating the lessons from her coaching sessions and courageously applying them in her real life.

Through her mentorship of Leah and her evolving conversations with Michael, Jil is no longer simply absorbing insights—she's living them. The shift is visible. The work is real. And the transformation has begun. Up until now, I've been walking Jil (and you) through reflection. But something powerful happens when you begin to ask these questions of yourself. From here forward, the Inner Compass Check-Ins will invite you to step into first-person — to own the questions not as something asked of you, but something you declare for yourself."

Anisa-ism™

"Living on purpose isn't about what you do—it's about how fully you show up in the doing."

Inner Compass Check-In:

- Where am I showing up out of obligation instead of intention?
- What's one area of my life I can shift from autopilot to alignment?
- What would a five-minute Purpose Pause create space for in my day?

Growth Assignment

Take five quiet minutes each morning (or before a big moment) to center yourself. Ask: *What would it look like to live/lead on purpose today?*

Chapter 11

Invest in Yourself

There's a difference between self-care and self-investment. Anisa made that clear from the jump.

"Self-care is a moment," she said. "Investment is a movement."

This session started quietly. Anisa handed me today's card from the LBLF deck: **"Your calendar isn't the only thing that needs a reset— your worth does too."**

I smiled. Then swallowed the lump forming in my throat.

She invited me to name the last time I did something solely for me— not for performance, not for parenting, not even for the paycheck. I couldn't remember.

And that's when it hit me. Tracey didn't assign me a coach because I was failing. She invested in me because she saw value I had forgotten. She believed in the leader I was beneath the burnout. And somewhere along the way, she'd learned what I was only now discovering:

"Your greatest Return on Investment(ROI) starts with
the courage to choose yourself."

We talked about how I'd been operating like a broken ATM— constantly dispensing energy and leadership without any deposits back into me.

Anisa reached beside her chair and pulled out a small round mirror—the kind with a wooden handle and a soft gold edge, worn slightly at the base from years of use. It wasn't flashy. But it felt sacred. Like it had witnessed a hundred breakthroughs before mine.

She handed it to me slowly, like she was offering more than just glass and metal.

"Let's try something," she said. "Look at yourself. Really look."

I hesitated, fingers tightening around the handle. I hadn't *really* looked at myself in a long time—beyond makeup checks and Zoom angles. Not like this.

But I raised it anyway.

My eyes met mine. Instinctively, I softened my face, adjusted my expression—like I always did. The performer in me was still present, still protective.

"Now," Anisa said, her voice steady, "read the words taped to the bottom."

I hadn't even noticed the small slip of paper tucked inside the frame until then.

I glanced down, then back at my own reflection.

"I am not the leftover," I read aloud, voice barely above a whisper.

"I am the legacy."

The words caught in my throat. My eyes didn't move. I stayed with myself.

Anisa waited. Gave me space. Didn't rush.

"Say it again," she said softly.

This time, I looked myself in the eye.

"I am not the leftover. I am the legacy."

Something shifted. The weight I'd been carrying—the years of invisible labor, of being everything for everyone, of feeling like I came last—suddenly felt seen. Not fixed. But named.

I stayed with my reflection for a few more breaths. My face didn't look different. But I felt different *inside* of it.

When I finally lowered the mirror, my hand trembled just slightly. I handed it back to Anisa, and she received it with both hands, like we were passing something holy between us.

She didn't say much after that.

She didn't need to.

The moment had already said enough.

As we were finishing up she asked me to list five ways I could start investing in myself this quarter. Not expensive things. Meaningful things. I wrote:

- Therapy.
- Walks without my phone.
- Dinner with friends where we don't talk about work.
- A solo staycation—just one night.
- Rejoining my book club (they still text me even though I ghosted them months ago).

Anisa nodded. "The moment you start pouring into yourself again, the whole system shifts."

She handed me a sample page from the LBLF Planner and pointed to the section labeled *Personal Investment Priorities.*

"It's not selfish," she said. "It's strategic."

I took the page, folded it gently, and tucked it in my purse behind a photo of Malik and Maya. Because this wasn't just about investing in me. It was about modeling for them what thriving could look like.

I used to think self-care was something you did *after* the work was done. After the deadline. After the dinner. After the third round of edits. After everyone else was okay.

Then I looked up and realized I'd spent years treating myself like an afterthought.

Anisa didn't ask me to add anything to my plate this week. She asked me to remove three things.

"Look at your commitments," she said, "and ask: *What's depleting you? What feels performative? What would you cancel right now if it didn't come with guilt?*"

I laughed in the moment. But when I sat with the question later, it stopped being funny.

I had built a whole life around what I *should* be doing. And somehow, I had abandoned the woman I could be becoming.

So I started small. I canceled a meeting that didn't need to happen. I blocked an hour and labeled it "Recharge." I said no to a last-minute "favor" that would've kept me up until midnight. And I took myself to a quiet little cafe on Saturday morning—with no laptop, no guilt, and no obligation to post about it.

The next session, Anisa asked me: **"What if your capacity is your most important KPI?"**

I sat with that. She leaned in.

"You're not paid for how much you can tolerate, Jil. You're paid for how clearly you can think, how wisely you can lead, and how well you can sustain it."

That last part got me. I'd been running on empty and expecting excellence. Pouring from a cracked cup and wondering why everything felt… fragile.

So I did something I hadn't done in months. I booked a massage. I signed up for the quiet yoga class—not the one that felt like punishment. I committed to using my LIFE journal. One that felt like an invitation.

This wasn't indulgence. It was integration.

I was remembering that I am a resource, too. And resources must be renewed, not just exploited.

Later that week, I was on a call with one of my high-potential directors. She sounded like I used to—exhausted, sharp, apologizing for being overwhelmed. I didn't give her strategy. I gave her permission.

"You don't have to bleed to prove you care," I said.

"Let's start protecting your energy like your leadership depends on it—because it does."

And just like that, I realized: I was becoming the kind of leader I wished I'd had.

Coaching Reflection

In this chapter, Jil discovered powerful truths about self-worth and the importance of prioritizing her own needs and desires.

Self-care sustains. Self-investment transforms. The return on investment from coaching, therapy, mentorship, and restorative practices is exponential—not just for your career, but for your life. You don't have to earn your replenishment; it is your right, not a reward.

Remember: **Your leadership is only as strong as your capacity.** Protect it. Nurture it. Honor the space you need to lead boldly and live fully.

Anisa-ism:

"You are a resource too. Pour wisely. Refill often."

Inner Compass Check-In:

- What have I been tolerating that's draining me?
- When's the last time I did something just for me—with no agenda?
- What does investing in myself *actually* look like in this season?

Growth Assignment

Personal Investment Priorities List—List three to five meaningful ways you can reinvest in your well-being and development this quarter. Include both internal (e.g., therapy, journaling) and external (e.g., coaching, learning, time boundaries) investments.

Chapter 12

Focus on What Fuels You

"Say it with me," Anisa said, sliding today's card across the table.

"Everything that drains you doesn't deserve your devotion."

I read it out loud. Quietly. Twice.

She smiled. "Now let's find your fuel."

We were deep in the LIFE Fulfillment Framework now—L for Live on Purpose, I for Invest in Yourself. And today? F for Focus on What Fuels You.

Anisa handed me a blank sheet of paper and asked me to draw a line down the middle. Left side: *What fuels me.*

Right side: *What drains me.*

Without overthinking, I started writing.

Fuels:

- Slow mornings
- Cooking with Maya
- Deep conversation
- Creating vision decks
- Jazz
- Silence

Drains:

- Reactive meetings
- Unspoken resentment with Michael
- Group chats that go nowhere

- Saying yes when I mean no

She nodded. "This is your real job description. To protect the fuel. And manage the drain."

Then she leaned back. "Tell me about a moment when you chose joy over obligation."

Without hesitation, I told her the story.

Back when Malik was in middle school, I used to drive him to school every morning—36.9 miles each way, from our home in Clarksville into DC.

One day, Michael asked why I didn't just hire someone. "You're not a rideshare driver, Jil," he said. "Why are you running yourself ragged?"

And I looked him dead in the eye and said: **"I don't have to take him. I get to."**

Yes, it was traffic and early mornings and half-eaten bagels, but it was also music, laughter, talks about everything and nothing. It was the sacred ordinary.

Anisa just nodded. "That's it. That's the whole point. You don't have to earn your joy with exhaustion."

She slid a new card across the table:

"Joy doesn't compete with success. It completes it."

We mapped out my upcoming week based on the fuel-drain list. Created "Focus Fridays."

Declined three standing meetings.

Made space for movement.

Anisa handed me a carefully wrapped box tied with a soft white ribbon. I wasn't expecting anything—not a gift, not a gesture. But as I loosened the bow and lifted the lid, I felt something in me already beginning to soften.

Inside, nestled side by side, were two items.

A candle, etched with the words: **"Live Inspired Fully Every Day."**

And a small tin of loose-leaf tea labeled simply: **"Replenish."**

There was a card tucked beneath them. I unfolded it slowly and read:

"You cannot pour from an empty vessel."

"Light your life with intention. Nourish it with care."

I turned the candle over in my hand, running my thumb across the engraving like it might imprint something into my skin.

Anisa smiled gently. "This isn't a reward for what you've achieved," she said. "It's a reminder of how you're meant to live."

I didn't expect to feel emotional—but there it was. That familiar tightness in my throat. I blinked fast, trying to push it back.

Because for the first time in a long time, I wasn't chasing success.

I was choosing something deeper.

I was choosing *myself.*

That night, for the first time in a long time, I fell asleep without a to-do list running through my head.

Because I was done proving.

And ready to start feeling.

The next morning, I was standing in line at Grounded Café—the same cozy spot where I first met Anisa—when my phone began buzzing and pinging.

I glanced down at the screen.

Another virtual panel.

Another "quick" strategy session.

Another "Can you just…"

Six months ago, I would've said yes to all of it without even thinking. Because I could. Because I was capable. Because I didn't want to be seen as difficult, ungrateful, or unavailable.

But now?

Now I didn't even flinch.

I clicked *Decline. Decline. Decline.*

And in those ordinary, defiant clicks, I felt something extraordinary: a lightness, like I had just reclaimed another small piece of myself.

The line moved forward. I looked up and really *saw* the café this time. The soft lighting. The smell of cinnamon and espresso. The way the morning sun spilled through the windows like an invitation to slow down.

Back then, I would've ordered something to go and rushed off to the next obligation.

Today?

"Large rooibos with almond milk," I told the barista.

"And make it to stay."

Because I wasn't rushing anymore.

I was learning how to be *right here*.

Anisa had said it months ago: **"Just because you can doesn't mean you should."**

She called it **The Capacity Reframe.**

"A high-capacity woman doesn't say yes to everything she can do. She reserves her time, energy, and attention for what fuels her—so she can lead with purpose, not resentment."

That one hit hard. Because I had been saying yes out of guilt, fear, and muscle memory. Not from alignment.

So I started making two lists:

- Column One: What Drains Me
- Column Two: What Fuels Me

The draining list came fast:

- Being the emotional buffer in every meeting
- Leading initiatives no one's committed to
- Fixing messes I didn't create
- Pretending I'm okay when I'm not

- Dimming my joy because other people are uncomfortable

Then I paused and let myself name the fuel:

- Coaching women who are rediscovering their voice
- Writing—just for me
- Deep conversations that don't need to go anywhere
- Time with my kids where I'm actually present
- Quiet mornings with candles and no agenda

When I looked at both lists, I felt something I hadn't felt in a long time: **clarity**.

"Leadership isn't just about what you do at work," Anisa said. **"It's how you choose what to carry—and what to release."**

So I started releasing. I handed off a project that was never mine to hold. I asked for help—without apologizing for it. I stopped explaining myself to people committed to misunderstanding me. And I started choosing joy again.

One afternoon, I went to Maya's orchestra performance.

Turned off my phone. No email. No Slack. No distractions.

Just Maya. Bow in hand. Glowing.

I watched her and thought:

This is fuel.

> *"This is the life I almost missed while chasing someone else's idea of success."*

Later that night, I texted Anisa:

Me: I said no three times this week. I said yes to joy twice.

Anisa: You're learning to lead yourself. That's the first yes that matters.

Coaching Reflection

In this chapter, Jil learned that leadership isn't just about what you accomplish—it's about what you choose to carry and what you choose to release. She discovered that protecting her energy isn't selfish; it's strategic. Everything that drains you doesn't deserve your devotion. Joy doesn't compete with success—it completes it. When you align your life with what fuels you, leadership stops feeling like a grind and starts feeling like a gift. And that's where real fulfillment begins.

Anisa-ism™

"You don't need permission to prioritize joy. You need clarity to protect it."

Inner Compass Check-In:

- Where am I giving away energy that doesn't align with my purpose?
- What would shift if I structured my week around what fuels me?
- What story am I telling myself about what I *have* to do—and is it true?

Growth Assignment

Fuel & Drain Inventory — Create your personal "Fuel vs. Drain" list. Use it weekly to recalibrate your schedule, reframe your yeses, and protect your capacity.

Chapter 13

Execute with Excellence

"This is the part most people skip," Anisa said, allowing me to pick up a card. **"It's not about the goal. It's the daily practice."**

I held the card in my hand, reading it over and over. Because I knew this was where I'd historically fallen short. Not in dreaming. Not in starting. But in sustaining.

This was the final leg of the LIFE Fulfillment Framework—L for Live on Purpose, I for Invest in Yourself, F for Focus on What Fuels You, and now, **E for Execute with Excellence**.

"I want to," I said. "But how do I actually stick to it?"

Anisa smiled. "Let's build your rhythm, not your fantasy."

She pulled out a sheet labeled "Execution Map." Across the top, it read: **"You own the time in your life—tell it where to go."**

We started with the one thing. Not 10 goals. Not a three-year vision. **Just one thing that mattered most in this season.**

For me, it was reclaiming my voice as a leader—not just executing deliverables but influencing culture.

"So let's reverse engineer that into daily practice," she said.

We broke it down like a 12-week sprint. Not a marathon—just a focused, repeatable run.

"What gets scheduled gets done," she reminded me. "Execution is how you build integrity with yourself."

She handed me another card:

"Clarity creates confidence. Structure sustains it."

For the next hour, we mapped out a framework that could flex with my life:

- Weekly goals tied to ONE priority
- Sunday Intentions
- Daily "Power Hour" of focused work—no distractions, no excuses
- Morning JAMMM™ reset: journal, affirm, meditate, mentally rehearse, and move
- Friday reflection: what worked, what drained, what needs to shift

It wasn't complicated. But it was intentional.

And suddenly, I didn't feel overwhelmed by my goals.

I felt grounded in my choices.

"Execution is devotion," Anisa said, "not just discipline."

She explained that excellence isn't about perfection. It's about consistency.

"It's not about doing *more*," she said. "It's about doing what *matters*—on purpose, and on repeat."

Then she dropped a truth bomb that I wrote in my journal in bold:

"Most people don't fail from lack of ambition. They fail from lack of alignment."

Then she added:

"Most people don't fail from a lack of information.
They fail from a lack of application."

That combination shifted me.

Because it wasn't about motivation—it was about systems. About becoming a woman whose habits match her highest vision.

I began implementing the LIFE Execution Map the following week. The first few days were bumpy. Life doesn't always follow your planner. But then, something clicked.

I stopped checking email before noon. I started ending my day with a 10-minute review. I built in buffer time to think—yes, *think*. Not just produce.

And I made peace with doing fewer things at a higher standard.

I heard Anisa's voice in my head: **"Create before you consume." "Honor your commitments to yourself." "The way you do one thing is the way you do everything."**

A few weeks in, my team noticed a shift.

"Your energy's different," one of my directors said. "Calmer. More focused."

I smiled. "I'm not chasing the fire anymore. I'm following the fuel."

The truth of that showed up in the very next meeting.

We were knee-deep in a project update when one of my managers began explaining why a deadline had been missed. The old me would have jumped in with solutions, peppered her with questions, or worse—taken the problem on myself. That day, though, I sat back, pen resting against my notebook, and listened. Really listened.

When she finished, instead of firing off my usual rapid response, I asked one simple question:

"What's the most important thing here—the fire or the fuel?"

The room went quiet. I could see the confusion flicker across a few faces. Then Marcus, my director of operations, leaned forward. "Wait… are you asking if this task is just putting out flames, or if it actually fuels our bigger goals?"

I nodded. "Exactly. Because if we're only chasing fires, we'll burn out. But if we can name what fuels us and organize around that, then even the hard work feels worth it."

Across the table, Priya broke into a grin. "That's different," she said. "Normally, you'd be halfway through fixing it yourself by now."

I laughed. "You're right. I used to carry it all, thinking leadership meant being the firefighter-in-chief. But I've realized it's not my job to carry every flame. It's my job to help us all see which sparks are worth tending, and which ones just burn energy we don't have to spare."

The team chuckled, and Marcus added, "So… you're saying not every fire drill deserves a fire truck?"

"Exactly," I said. "And definitely not my fire truck."

We spent the next ten minutes re-mapping the project—not around what was urgent, but around what was important. I could feel the energy in the room shift. People leaned in, ideas flowed, and for the first time in a long time, it didn't feel like we were scrambling. It felt like we were steering.

As the meeting wrapped, Nia spoke up again. "You're teaching us a new rhythm, Jil. I didn't realize how much we'd been running until you slowed us down enough to see it."

I left that meeting with more than an action plan. I left with proof that the changes I was making weren't just about me. They were shaping the culture of my team.

And that was the fuel I needed to keep going.

That night, after the meeting, I came home to the sound of music pulsing from upstairs. Malik had officially entered his "I'm-a-producer" phase. Which meant my once-quiet evenings were now soundtracked by bass beats shaking the walls.

I dropped my bag by the door and called up the stairs, "Do I need earplugs, or is this a family concert?"

His voice boomed back. "Both!"

I laughed and kicked off my heels. For months, I'd been so consumed with work that these moments barely registered. I'd walk in, half-listening, still scrolling through emails, already worried about tomorrow's meetings. Tonight, though, something was different. My calendar wasn't running me ragged anymore. I actually had energy left over. Space to notice. Space to play.

I padded upstairs and pushed open his door. Malik was hunched over his laptop, headphones slightly askew, nodding like he was the next Pharrell.

"Okay, Maestro," I said, crossing my arms. "Let me hear it."

He grinned, pressed a few keys, and suddenly the room exploded with sound. Heavy bass, layered claps, a catchy hook. Then — out of nowhere — a woman's voice singing the line: *'Stop chasing fire, follow the fuel.'*

I froze. "Wait. Is that… me?"

Malik burst out laughing. "Yep. I sampled you. You said it in the kitchen last week when I was stressing about homework."

I clapped a hand over my mouth, half mortified, half amazed. "You turned my mom advice into a track?"

"Mom," he said, dead serious, "it slaps."

I doubled over, laughing until my sides hurt. In that moment, the joy washed over me — not just because Malik had a sense of humor, but because I realized he'd been listening. Really listening. Even when I thought my words were just floating past him, they'd landed. Enough to make it into his music.

I sank onto his bed, still laughing, still catching my breath. "Well," I said, wiping tears from my eyes, "at least one of us is going platinum."

He grinned and handed me the headphones. "Nah, Mom. This is a collab."

And just like that, sitting in Malik's messy room with bass rattling the windows, I felt more connected than I had in months. Not the polished, perfect kind of connection I used to chase with networking dinners or leadership offsites. The messy, loud, real kind that fills you up without asking you to prove a thing.

As I walked out later, humming my own sampled voice, I realized something: this — this joy, this laughter, this reminder that I was more than my calendar — was fuel, too. The kind I hadn't made space for in far too long.

That month, I completed three strategic initiatives that had been lingering on my to-do list for over a year. Not because I was grinding harder. But because I was aligned.

I made fewer decisions. I trusted my plan. I protected my capacity.

And every Friday, I celebrated the practice—not just the progress. Sometimes that meant grabbing Maya for tacos at our favorite little spot down the street. She'd slide into the booth, phone in one hand, eyes scanning the room the way I used to when I was her age—already clocking the outfits, already noting who had style and who didn't.

"Mom, those boots?" she whispered once, tilting her head toward a woman across the restaurant. "That's a *look*."

I couldn't help but laugh. "You've got the eye," I said, leaning in like we were fashion editors at lunch instead of mother and daughter sharing guacamole. Truth was, I saw myself in her—the way she lingered over details, the way her face lit up when she noticed someone's confidence in what they wore. Fashion had always been my outlet, my little rebellion and my joy. And now here it was blooming in her too, right in front of me.

After tacos, we'd sometimes swing by Trader Joe's. I'd let her pick the flowers. She always chose boldly—bright ranunculus, oversized sunflowers, once even a spiky purple thistle that she insisted would look "artsy" on the table. And she was right. We'd get home, unwrap the paper, and arrange them together—me coaching her on trimming the stems, her coaching me on placement. "Not too symmetrical, Mom. It needs to look effortless."

I'd step back, and there she'd be—laughing, fussing, taking pride in how the kitchen came alive with just a vase of flowers and her touch.

Those Fridays weren't about crossing things off a list. They weren't about progress measured in deliverables or deadlines. They were about practice—practicing presence, practicing joy, practicing connection. Small rituals, simple joys.

Because that was the real win.

In this chapter of my life, I wasn't just leading teams. I was leading me.

And for the first time… it felt excellent.

I texted Anisa:

Me: I've stopped sprinting. I've started showing up.

Anisa: And that's where the magic lives.

Coaching Reflection

In this chapter, Jil discovered that excellence isn't about perfection or doing more—it's about alignment. By grounding her goals in daily rhythms instead of lofty intentions, she shifted from a time-starved executive chasing urgency to an intentional leader living her priorities. Execution became less about willpower and more about systems: weekly goals tied to one priority, daily rituals that fueled focus, and small practices that built integrity with herself.

Excellence flows from clarity. And clarity creates confidence, while structure sustains it. When Jil stopped sprinting and started honoring her capacity, she not only advanced strategic initiatives at work but also rediscovered joy at home—with Malik in the studio, Maya over tacos, and fresh flowers on the table.

Excellence, she learned, isn't a finish line. It's devotion to the choices that reflect who you are becoming. One aligned step at a time—that's where the magic lives.

Anisa-ism™

"It's not about the goal. It's the daily practice."

Inner Compass Check-In:

- Where in your life have you been sprinting instead of sustaining?

- What's the one priority in this season that deserves your daily devotion?
- Which system, ritual, or rhythm could you create to help you follow through when motivation fades?
- How are you honoring your capacity instead of overextending it?
- What small practice, repeated with intention, would begin to shift everything?

Growth Assignment

LIFE Execution Map — Use this weekly tool to identify your *ONE priority*, plan your daily practices, and reflect on what's working. The goal is not perfection, but rhythm.

- **Set Your ONE Priority**: Choose the single outcome that matters most in this season. Write it clearly at the top of your map.
- **Sunday Intentions**: Block 30 minutes to plan your week. Anchor every goal and activity to your ONE priority.
- **Daily Power Hour**: Schedule one focused, distraction-free hour each day to move your priority forward. Protect it.
- **Morning JAMMM™ Reset**: Journal, Affirm, Move, Meditate, Map your day. Build consistency through ritual.
- **Friday Reflection**: Ask yourself: *What worked? What drained me? What needs to shift?* Use these insights to refine your next week.

Optional bonus: Share your ONE priority with a trusted peer, coach, or mentor. Accountability is love.

Chapter 14

Coming Home

The shift didn't happen all at once. It arrived in waves—quiet realizations that crept in between coffee refills and calendar invites.

Little moments that would've slipped past me before were now loud with insight. I was becoming someone who noticed.

I caught myself before saying yes out of guilt. I paused when Maya asked for help instead of sighing. I felt my shoulders drop when I stopped overexplaining in meetings.

This was what Anisa meant by awareness—not just noticing what was wrong but choosing what's right.

"Awareness is the beginning of authority," she'd said. And it was true. Once I could see myself clearly, I could start to lead myself better.

That week, I took a long walk through Rock Creek Park—just me, my sneakers, and the sounds of spring trying to push through a late DC winter. I thought about the choices I had made over the years that led me here.

Some of them were survival. Some of them were strategy. But now? I was choosing based on alignment. Not urgency. Not ego. Not fear.

Anisa and I started using a new phrase: **Aligned over automatic.** And I could feel the difference. In the way I led. In the way I listened. In the way I returned to myself after conflict.

One afternoon, Tracey pulled me aside. "I don't know what Anisa is doing," she said with a small smile. "But whatever it is… it's working."

I thanked her. Not performatively. Not out of politeness. From a grounded, grateful place. Because I was no longer leading from depletion. I was leading from awareness. And aligning from the inside out.

Anisa's latest card now lived on my fridge at home: **"Clarity is not loud. It's steady."** And so was I.

I thought restoring myself would look like a breakthrough. A movie moment. A teary confession. A big, dramatic return to the woman I used to be.

But it was quieter than that. It was breakfast with Malik—just the two of us. No lectures. No hovering. Just eggs. And space.

And a 16-year-old son who, for the first time in months, looked up from his plate and said: **"You seem... happier."**

That was it. That was the reconciliation.

It was Maya humming in the car again. Not asking for anything. Just humming. It was the conversation with Michael where we sat on the porch and didn't fix anything. Didn't promise anything. Just named the truth between us.

"We're both evolving," I said. "And I don't want to pretend we're the same people who said 'I do' 18 years ago."

He nodded. "We're not."

Silence. But it wasn't painful this time. It was honest. Clean. Clear.

At work, coming home to myself looked like handing a project off without guilt. Like mentoring a young leader and telling her, **"You don't have to lose yourself to lead well. Trust me—I tried that."**

It was the moment my team surprised me with a card. Nothing fancy. No fanfare. Just a handwritten note that said: **"Thanks for showing up as yourself. It makes it easier for us to do the same."**

For the first time in months, tears were flowing. Not because I was tired. But because I wasn't.

Anisa and I sat in her office a week later for what was technically our final session. She asked, "What's different now?"

I say *technically* because I knew the truth: Anisa wasn't just a coach I'd worked with for a season. From now on—and for as long as I keep leading and living—she would be a trusted advisor, a voice of clarity I could return to again and again as I navigated my career and my life.

I let the question settle, thinking for a minute. "Everything feels the same," I said finally. "But I'm in it now. Fully."

She smiled. "That's what reconciliation looks like, Jil. Not fixing everything. Just showing up for it with clarity and compassion."

I looked down at the journal she gave me during our first session. I flipped back to the first page—the one where I wrote: **"I don't even know who I am anymore."**

And now? I knew.

I'm Jil. VP. Leader. Mother. Woman. Not perfect. But present. Not fixed. But found.

Anisa's last words to me were: *"You were not searching for something out there. You were remembering something in here."*

As she spoke, she pressed her hand against her own heart and held my eyes. My throat tightened. My eyes stung.

Then Anisa said softly:

In the soil of your own life, everything you've been longing for has been quietly waiting—waiting for you to name it, to notice it, and to nourish it into the fullness it was always meant to become.

It was here all along.

In your breath.

In your spirit.

In the quiet corners of your own backyard, waiting for you to see the diamonds beneath your feet.

You were never broken.

You were simply being called home.

Coaching Reflection

In this chapter, Jil discovered that coming home to herself wasn't a grand event—it was a series of small, steady choices. She learned that awareness is the beginning of true authority, and alignment, not urgency, is the path to sustainable leadership. She realized that fulfillment isn't something you chase—it's something you reclaim. The life she was longing for wasn't somewhere out there; it had been quietly waiting within her all along, ready to be named, noticed, nurtured, and lived.

Anisa-ism™

"Burnout is what happens when you chase success. Breakthrough is what happens when you choose yourself."

Inner Compass Check-In:

- What has shifted in me since I began this journey?
- Where have I stopped performing and started becoming?
- What does "coming home to myself" look like in this next season?

Growth Assignment

The Alignment Audit — Reflect on three areas of your life (work, relationships, self). Where are you leading from depletion? Where are you leading from alignment?

Chapter 15

The Next Chapter

I didn't realize I had changed until the world started responding to me differently. It wasn't dramatic. No sudden promotion. No massive announcement. Just a different rhythm. A new way of breathing.

I started taking morning walks—not to burn calories or check off a habit tracker, but to listen. To God. To myself. To the quiet wisdom rising in the stillness.

I carried a journal in my bag, full of Anisa-isms, prayers, and bold questions that no longer scared me. Not questions like "What's next?" But deeper ones: **"What's aligned?" "What's mine to carry?" "What's ready to be released?"**

At our final session, Anisa smiled before I even sat down. "You don't look lighter because your schedule changed," she said. **"You look lighter because you changed."**

She handed me one final card: **"The most important project you'll ever lead… is yourself."**

We sat in the stillness together. Two women, one journey, one truth: I had come home to myself.

Then she asked, "What's your next chapter?"

And this time, I didn't hedge. I didn't overthink. I didn't list deliverables or bullet-point a strategy.

I spoke from a place I had fought to reclaim: "Whatever it is—it will be on my terms. Built on purpose. Grounded in joy. And bold enough to leave a legacy."

Anisa stood. Wrapped me in a hug. "You'll still have hard days. But now, you'll have tools. Truth. And a tribe- the people who will remind you who you are when you forget."

I left her office and headed straight to Leah's. We had a vision board date planned at her new home. She and her husband had moved to prepare for the baby. She had texted earlier that week: **You've inspired me. I want to lead differently.**

Later that evening, Michael and I sat on the porch holding hands at our home. No phones. Just a quiet closeness we hadn't felt in months. We didn't need to fix everything. We just needed to show up.

And that night, I wrote in my journal: **"You don't have to start over. You just have to start now."**

The next chapter wasn't a title or a milestone. It was Maya humming in the car again. It was breakfast with Malik—just the two of us. It was a calm conversation with Tracey that didn't end in action items, but in alignment. It was lighting a candle, taking a breath, and trusting that peace is a strategy too.

It wasn't flashy. But it was mine.

Because the next chapter isn't something you wait for. It's something you *walk into.* With open eyes. With unclenched hands. With your whole self.

I've stopped performing. And I've started becoming.

It feels like peace.

It feels like purpose.

It feels like me.

Coaching Reflection

In this chapter, Jil realized that the next chapter of her life wasn't something she had to chase—it was something she chose to create. She learned that peace is a strategy, alignment is a strength, and becoming is more powerful than performing. Leading herself first became the foundation for leading others well. Her breakthrough wasn't a destination—it was a way of being. The next chapter didn't need to be bigger. It needed to be hers.

Activation Card

"You don't have to start over. You just have to start now."

Inner Compass Check-In:

- Where have I already started becoming who I was searching for?
- What's the new rhythm I want to walk in?
- If I could build my life around peace and purpose, what would I say yes to next?

Because the next chapter doesn't begin when everything is figured out. It begins the moment you show up as who you really are.

And I'm ready.

Growth Assignment

Next Chapter Vision Ritual—Spend 20 minutes journaling or vision boarding using the prompts:

- What does peace feel like for me?
- What do I want to create—not just achieve?
- What am I no longer willing to sacrifice for success?

Epilogue: From Anisa

To every leader who found themselves in Jil's story—this was written for you.

I've had the honor of coaching hundreds of leaders over the years—some industry veterans, some rising stars, all of them deeply capable and quietly exhausted. What I've learned is that Jil isn't just a character. Jil is a composite of the real people I've sat across from in coaching rooms, on executive retreats, and in moments of breakdown and breakthrough. Some of them were women. Many were men. All were navigating what it means to succeed outwardly while questioning inwardly:

"Is this what success is supposed to feel like?"

That question is what compelled me to write this book.

Because I believe leadership is not just about performance. It's about presence. It's not just about goals. It's about grounding. It's not just about titles. It's about truth.

You deserve to lead from a place of alignment—not anxiety. You deserve a strategy that doesn't sacrifice your soul. And you don't have to figure it all out alone.

At ARE Global Solutions, we partner with executives in fast-paced, high-growth organizations to develop world-class leaders, build inclusive environments, and design coaching and development experiences that drive results without burning people out.

Our belief is simple: **You don't have to choose between success and fulfillment.**

"You're meant to have both. Because burnout happens when you chase success."

"Breakthrough happens when you choose yourself."

Through executive coaching, AI advisory, CMMC compliance solutions, transformational retreats, luxury travel experiences, curated events, and invitation-only dining experiences, we help leaders—just like you—Lead BOLDLY™ and Live FULLY™.

At the heart of our work are two signature frameworks:

The BOLD Leadership Framework™

A roadmap for leading with Vision, Intention, and Impact:
- **B** – Believe Boldly
- **O** – Organize Strategically
- **L** – Lead with Intention
- **D** – Drive Results

The LIFE Fulfillment Framework™
A compass for designing a life of sustainable success:
- **L** – Live on Purpose
- **I** – Invest in Yourself
- **F** – Focus on What Fuels You
- **E** – Execute with Excellence

Together, these frameworks are more than models—they are mirrors, helping you return to your highest self and move forward with clarity and courage.

So if you saw yourself in Jil... If you've been leading on autopilot... If you're ready to reconnect with your purpose, your power, and your people...

Let's talk.

And if you don't know where to start? That's okay.

Start with a conversation at CEO@AREGlobalSolutions.com.

Visit www.areglobalsolutions.com or call us directly.

You don't have to do this alone. You just have to decide you're ready.

Here's to your next chapter.

With deep respect and unwavering belief in who you're becoming,

Anisa Rashad

Founder & CEO, ARE Global Solutions

Creator of the Lead BOLDLY. Live FULLY™ Framework

Resources & Acknowledgements

RESOURCES

Whether you are just starting your leadership journey or deepening your commitment to lead with vision, intention, and impact—these resources are here to support your continued growth.

"Lead BOLDLY. Live FULLY™ Planner"

A guided planning system designed to help you integrate the BOLD and LIFE frameworks into your everyday routines. Available at www.leadboldlylivefully.net

"LBLF Anisa-isms Activation Cards"

36 cards to inspire clarity, courage, and sustainable self-leadership. Each card includes a powerful truth to anchor your week.

The BOLD Leadership Framework™ + LIFE Fulfillment Framework™ One-Pagers

Download printable visuals that outline the signature frameworks introduced in this book.

ARE Global Solutions Coaching and Retreats

Explore executive coaching, strategic advising, and transformational retreats for individuals and organizations. Learn more at www.areglobalsolutions.com

Lead BOLDLY Collective™

A curated community of high-achieving, soul-aligned leaders. Invitations to workshops, summits, and curated conversations for connection and growth.

Not sure where to begin?

Schedule a Connection, Clarity & Commitment Call with our team: www.areglobalsolutions.com

ACKNOWLEDGEMENTS

This book would not exist without the courage and vulnerability of the countless leaders I've coached—many of whom live in the DNA of Jil's story.

To every woman who stayed too long in a place that no longer fit… to every man who quietly carried pressure and pretended it was peace… to every leader who succeeded in public but questioned everything in private—thank you for trusting me with your truth. You gave this book its heart.

To my ARE Global Solutions team—you embody the mission. Your brilliance, care, and excellence are behind every program, every conversation, every breakthrough. I'm proud to build with you.

To my children, my heartbeats—you are my why. Watching you grow has made me braver, softer, and more intentional in how I lead and live.

To the visionary leaders who will rise through these pages—I see you. I believe in you. You are not alone.

And finally, to the reader holding this book: Thank you for choosing yourself. Thank you for leading with courage. Thank you for beginning again.

With gratitude and purpose,

Anisa Rashad

Founder & CEO, ARE Global Solutions

Creator of the Lead BOLDLY. Live FULLY™ Framework

Reflection Questions

Use these prompts for personal journaling, team discussions, or coaching conversations.

- Where in your life or leadership have you been performing instead of embodying?
- What's one area where you need to become more of a TEAM (Time, Energy, Attention Manager)?
- What drains you—and how can you start saying no to it?
- What fuels you—and how can you intentionally create more space for it?
- What does success *feel* like to you—not just look like?
- What ripple do you want your leadership to leave behind?

Visionary Closeout from Anisa

Beautiful Leader,

You made it to the end—but this is only the beginning.

The story you just read isn't just about Jil.

It's about all of us who've ever smiled through the pressure, performed through the exhaustion, or succeeded while slowly disappearing from ourselves.

You don't have to do that anymore.

You can lead differently. You can live fully.

Let *this* be the moment you remember your time is sacred. Your joy is strategic. Your voice is powerful.

You are the most important project you'll ever lead.

And you don't have to do it alone.

If you—or someone you lead—could benefit from coaching, curated retreats, or bold strategic support…

Let's connect. I built **ARE Global Solutions** for leaders like you. **Visit:** www.LeadBoldlyLiveFully.net

I can't wait to meet the next version of you.

With love, power, and purpose,

Anisa Rashad, MBA

Founder & CEO, ARE Global Solutions

Turn the Page → Sneak Preview of Book 2

Before you go, I'd like to give you a glimpse of what's next in the *Lead BOLDLY. Live FULLY*™ series.

Every breakthrough creates a ripple. Jil's transformation doesn't just change her life—it begins to shift the world around her, especially at home. Her husband, Michael Harrington, is a man who seems unstoppable on the outside but carries a very different story on the inside.

Here's your exclusive preview of *Book 2: The Pressure Principle. A Leadership Fable for Leaders Who Built Success on Fragile Foundations*

"Because pressure shouldn't be the price of success."

Chapter One — The Beginning of Pressure
The house glowed with the warmth of Christmas lights, laughter weaving through every corner as carols played softly in the background. Michael stood near the front door, half-listening to a colleague tell a story, but his eyes kept drifting across the room.
There she was. Jil.
She stood near the fireplace, radiant in a red dress, a glass of sparkling cider in her hand. Her body language was open, alive, magnetic. A small circle surrounded her—friends, neighbors, colleagues—and every head was tilted her way. They were laughing, nodding, hanging on her words.
Michael felt something stir inside him. She wasn't just speaking. She was holding court. And she wasn't performing this time. She wasn't forcing it. She was herself. Fully herself.
He exhaled, a smile tugging at the corner of his mouth. She made it back, he thought. After all the exhaustion, the doubt, the weight she carried, she had found her way home to herself.
And then, almost as quickly, the thought turned inward.
But what about me?
The champagne glass in his hand suddenly felt heavier. The room felt louder. The pressure he lived with every day—the targets, the deals,

the endless need to perform—pressed harder against his chest. From the outside, he looked like the man who had it all. But inside? He knew the truth.

He watched Jil laugh again, her head thrown back, joy spilling into the room like light. And for the first time in months, Michael wondered if there was another way. A way to loosen the grip of fear. A way to breathe again. A way to find peace—not just with Jil, but within himself.

His hand slipped into his pocket, fingers brushing against his phone. He thought of Anisa, of the quiet authority she carried, the way Jil spoke about her like a compass pointing true north.

After the new year, he told himself. I'm calling her. I think it's time.

He looked back at Jil—his wife, his mirror, his reminder of what was possible. And though the room buzzed with celebration, Michael stood in a different kind of moment. A beginning.

"From across the room, Jil felt his eyes on her."

She turned, laughter still on her lips, and met Michael's gaze. For a moment, the party noise faded. She saw the pride in his expression, yes — but also the pressure he carried in his shoulders, the worry lines that were becoming etched into his face.

And then it struck her — as clear as the angel his mother had given them before she passed, the one perched at the very top of their tree — Michael needed to find his way home.